THE TRIUNE NATURE OF GOD:

CONVERSATIONS REGARDING THE TRINITY BY A DISCIPLES OF CHRIST PASTOR/THEOLOGIAN

Topical Line Drives
Volume 37

ROBERT CORNWALL, PH.D.

Energion Publications
Gonzalez, Florida
2019

Cover Design: Henry E. Neufeld

ISBN: 978-1-63199-697-9

Energion Publications
PO Box 841
Gonzalez, FL 32560

http://www.energion.com
pubs@energion.com

INTRODUCTION

Traditionally, Christians have spoken of God in trinitarian terms. There is disagreement as to when this understanding of God emerged. The word Trinity is not found in Scripture, but one can find patterns that support a trinitarian vision of God in Scripture. A definitive statement concerning the Trinity emerged out of the Council of Nicaea in 325 CE, though the Creed that churches use to confess a trinitarian understanding of God did not reach its final form until the Council of Constantinople met in 381 CE. While traditions confessing their faith using the Nicene Creed have expressed this faith in trinitarian terms, that does not mean everyone has had the same understanding of the Trinity. In fact, adherence to the belief that God is Trinity has ebbed and flowed, especially after the beginning of the Enlightenment. For some at least, this doctrine of the Trinity has been deemed illogical and irrational. To those who struggle with the Trinity, it might be better to affirm the oneness of God and embrace the humanity of Jesus. As for the Holy Spirit, well the Spirit has often been the subject of neglect. The Apostles' Creed only expresses belief in the Holy Spirit, with no definition of terms. The Nicene Creed does go further, probably due to the influence of the Cappadocian Fathers. While the Nicene Creed gave official definition to a trinitarian understanding of God, using the Greek word *homoousious* to affirm that while Father, Son, and Holy Spirit are three persons, they share one substance or one essence, not everyone fully embraced this understanding. A number of church leaders of that age preferred other terms, including *homoiousious*, which speaks of "like substance," instead of *homoousious*. In the end, the majority of those church leaders who formed the homoiousious party affirmed the position espoused by the homoousious party. Thus, they also affirmed the form of the Creed that has come down to us.

Constantinople did not end the debate over the triune nature of God— further discussion would ensue regarding the way in which the Christ was both divine and human, as well as fully understanding the nature of the Holy Spirit—but a foundation was laid upon which those conversations could be undertaken. The majority of the debates that followed would involve clarification of this doctrine, but there would not be any wholesale changes to the doctrine. Thus, from Constantinople forward the church in east and west confessed that God is at once three persons who share one substance or essence. As for the nature of this essence/substance, there might be differing opinions, but the affirmation has held into the twenty-first century.

The debate over the triune nature of God has Christological roots. It is an expression of the church's felt need to define Jesus' relationship to God. If Jesus is the Son of God, what does that mean? For Christians who embrace the Nicene Creed, one can confess that the Christ is "the only Son of God, eternally begotten of the Father, God from God, Light from Light, true God from true God, begotten, not made, of *one substance* with the Father; through him all things were made." Whether one completely understands this confession, one can go forth with the assumption that in some fashion Jesus is divine, while affirming monotheism. But, what if a person is not a creedal Christian? How might such a person understand the confession found in Mark 1:1 that Jesus Christ is the Son of God? This a key question that deserves our attention. In what way is Jesus the Son of God? Does this entail some sense of divinity? Or, is Jesus a human being who has been adopted by God the Father as God's son? In addition, there is the question of the status of the Holy Spirit. Is the Holy Spirit a person within the Godhead, or is the Spirit simply a way of designating Gods' presence in the world, a mode of being? The Creed assumes that what applies to Christ applies to the Holy Spirit, "who with the Father and the Son is worshiped and glorified."

The fourth-century church leaders and theologians whose re-flections led to the formation of the creed may not have been in full agreement as to the meaning of the word *homoousious,* but they accepted it in the interest of unity (many preferred the term *homoiousious,* or "like substance"). With the Creed in place, a base-line for speaking of God was laid, though the question of Christ's full divinity and full humanity remained unresolved, at least until Chalcedon in the mid-fifth-century. These creedal statements may not be perfect, but they served to create a foundation for further theological clarification. One might have questions about the meaning of the creed, but confessionally it helped set theological parameters for most Christians.

With this booklet, which focuses on the doctrine of the Trinity, I hope to initiate a conversation concerning the Trinity both within my tradition as well as outside it. This effort emerged out of anoth-er project, in which I am seeking to provide a guide to theology for members of my tribe, the Christian Church (Disciples of Christ). I serve this tradition as a pastor, historian, and theologian (my Ph.D. is in historical theology). While the Disciples do not have an official creed, I am by confession a trinitarian Christian. That is, I am willing to affirm the definition of God found in the Nicene Creed, even if my understanding of the details might differ from others who make the same confession. At the same time, as a Dis-ciple, I cannot and will not make the Creed or belief in the Trinity a test of fellowship. Since we are a non-creedal community, such a requirement would be difficult to implement, but it would also be a self-defeating effort. It will do nothing to convince non-trinitarians of the value of this long-held doctrine of the church.

While we are non-creedal that doesn't mean we are anti-theo-logical. It simply means greater weight is given to Scripture than to later developments. Thus, Barton Stone, who was one of the founders of the Stone-Campbell Movement, of which the Disci-ples are but one branch, would accept as true only that which is provable from Scripture. Since the term Trinity is not found in

Scripture, members of this faith community will need to agree to disagree on what some of us believe is an important matter of Christian theology. Another way of putting this is to say that while we are noncreedal, that does not mean that everyone within the Disciples community rejects the testimony of the historic creeds. It does mean that affirming the message of these creeds is a personal decision, not one imposed from on high.[1]

With this preface, it should come as no surprise that within the Disciples community there is no unanimity regarding belief in the Trinity. That includes both the denomination and the congregation I serve. There are Disciples who embrace the doctrine, and Disciples who do not. This has been true for us from the earliest days of the Stone-Campbell Movement. Writing early in the twentieth century, Edward Scribner Ames, a leading liberal Disciples theologian, could write that the meaning of the doctrine of the Trinity was never very clear, and that "the doctrines of the Trinity have little significance for our time." Why? Because "they are not demanded by our moral life and they are not taught by the Scriptures. Therefore, they may be allowed to pass with the intellectual world to which they belonged."[2] While the doctrine emerged in large part due to questions about Jesus' relationship with God, Ames believed these questions were the concern of an earlier age that had long passed. They have nothing to say to modern concerns. Testimonies to the birth and death of Jesus are nothing more than "the record of the wonder-love of the human heart, which continues to make legendary narratives about very human men."[3] Ames wrote this before the renaissance of trinitarian thinking that is generally attributed to Karl Barth, but Ames' view is consistent with much current Disciples thinking on the subject.

1   Robert D. Cornwall, *Freedom in Covenant: Reflections on the Distinctive Values and Practices of the Christian Church (Disciples of Christ)*, (Eugene, OR: Wipf & Stock Publishers, 2015), pp. 8-9.
2   Edward Scribner Ames, *The New Orthodoxy*, (Chicago: The University of Chicago Press, 1918), pp. 45-46.
3   Ames, *New Orthodoxy*, p. 46.

What follows is an invitation to Disciples, and others who struggle with the doctrine of the Trinity, to enter a conversation about the Trinity. I do not intend for this brief book to be taken as an imposition of a trinitarian vision on the Stone-Campbell Movement as a whole or on the Disciples branch in particular. However, I strongly believe that the doctrine of the Trinity can enhance one's vision of God. I agree with Leonard Allen, a Church of Christ theologian, who writes that that "the explicit doctrine of the Trinity that gradually emerged in the first four centuries was not simply a philosophical construct imposed back upon Scripture but rather a result of the necessary work of filling out the New Testament's pervasive triadic language about God as the gospel mission engaged Greco-Roman culture."[4]

Since this book emerged from a larger theological project meant to stir theological conversation within my own ecclesial community, I offer it up to Disciples and the Christian community at large as an invitation to think deeply about the theological foundations of the Christian faith. That is, this is my invitation to fellow Disciples (and others) to move along the path of faith toward understanding, knowing that full understanding will never come to us in this life. As Paul reminds us, we are simply viewing reality as if a reflection in a mirror (1 Cor. 13: 12).

This journey of discovery will include engaging in conversations with members of the Stone-Campbell tradition, especially Alexander Campbell and Barton Stone. We will also engage the biblical record, for that is in keeping with the tradition of my people. We will also spend some time looking at the development over time of trinitarian vocabulary as well as historical efforts to understand and define the nature of God as Trinity. In the course of the journey I will engage with Disciple theologians, especially Clark Williamson and Joe Jones, but also theologians from outside the movement, especially Elizabeth Johnson and Catherine

---

4   Leonard Allen, *Poured Out: The Spirit of God Empowering the Mission of God,* (Abilene, TX: Abilene Christian University Press, 2018), p. 63.

Mowry LaCugna—both of whom are Roman Catholic feminist theologians—whose work I have found helpful. As the conversation moves to a close I want to pose the question of whether having creeds is a necessary step in our ability to speak faithfully as Christians about God. I realize this will seem counter-intuitive, but I wonder whether we would be better off to affirm, at the very least, the confession of Constantinople as a sign of our ecumenical commitments.

Again, I write this book as a Disciple pastor and theologian, with Disciples in mind. While Disciples are my primary audience, because we struggle with, and often shy away from, this conversation, I know we are not alone. In part, this is because many Christians find the Trinity to be an incomprehensible doctrine. Even within strongly trinitarian communities there is a tendency to either embrace tri-theism (three gods) or modalism (one god who is experienced in three modes of being). It is no wonder that Barton Stone threw up his hands in bewilderment, declaring that the doctrine was completely illogical. So, whether you are a Disciple, a member of the Stone-Campbell Movement, or some other tradition, I invite you to join me on this journey of discovery regarding the Trinity. Perhaps you will join me in embracing a trinitarian understanding of God's nature, or perhaps not. That is your prerogative (at least from a Disciples perspective). Whether you embrace the doctrine or not, I think it's incumbent upon us to try to understand the issues at hand.

Chapter 1:

Disciples, Creeds, and the Trinity

Although most Christian communities make use of the historic creeds, including the Nicene Creed, to present to the world and to themselves the basic tenets of the Christian faith, not all Christians are so inclined. The Stone Campbell Movement, the heirs of Thomas and Alexander Campbell, together with Barton Stone, is one tradition that has sought to live without creeds and statements of faith that go beyond Scripture. This movement has traditionally sought to root its faith in the biblical testimony; more specifically in the New Testament. This tradition emerged out of the American frontier context, as well as the British Enlightenment. With Enlightenment thinkers such as John Locke, this tradition affirms the principle of freedom in matters of religion.[5] This tradition has taken the principle of *sola scriptura* and the principle of the priesthood of all believers quite seriously, rejecting the authoritative use of what have been deemed human-made creeds as well as a clerical hierarchy.

When it comes to the doctrine of the Trinity, adherents of the Stone-Campbell Movement have exhibited much ambivalence. There are Trinitarians within the movement, including both Thomas and Alexander Campbell, but as the late Disciples historian and church leader, Ronald Osborn, notes:

> The Disciples regarded themselves as neither Trinitarian nor Unitarian. Alexander Campbell would not use the term Trinitarian because it did not appear in scripture. He even changed one line in the great Trinitarian hymn, "Holy, Holy,

5   Robert D. Cornwall, *Freedom in Covenant: Reflections on the Distinctive Values and Practices of the Christian Church (Disciples of Christ)*, (Eugene, OR: Wipf & Stock Publishers, 2015), pp. 1-10.

Holy," so that instead of saying "God in three persons, blessed Trinity," people would sing, "God over all, and blest eternally.[6]

Although Osborn's assertion about the possible alteration of the hymn "Holy, Holy, Holy," seems difficult to prove, Campbell was reticent to use trinitarian language. Nevertheless, he was Trinitarian in his theology. Of his fellow reformer, Barton Stone, the same cannot be said. In fact, Stone not only declared that the word Trinity was not biblical, he made it clear that he wasn't a trinitarian (on the other hand, he also denied being a Unitarian).[7] He "wondered why Trinitarians are so tenacious of a doctrine, so feebly supported by scriptural authority."[8] Perhaps due to their rejection of what both Campbell and Stone believed were human creeds, the Movement that emerged from their ministries chose not to make an affirmation of the doctrine of the Trinity a test of fellowship. As Stone declared, if the doctrine is so important, "is it not very strange that it had not been so explicitly taught by the great Head of the church, that at least, its advocates could state the doctrine in some form, in which they themselves could agree."[9]

While I am a Disciples minister, historian, and theologian, who recognizes this ambivalence in our tradition, I am not ambivalent about the Trinity. I have fully embraced a trinitarian understanding of God, but I will confess that I do not draw this conviction from my life as a Disciple. My embrace of the Trinity is rooted in other experiences in the church, having recited the

---

6   Ronald Osborn, *The Faith We Affirm: Basic Beliefs of Disciples of Christ,* (St. Louis: Chalice Press, 1979), p. 52. Regarding the suggestion that Campbell replaced the trinitarian language from the hymn "Holy, Holy, Holy," and replaced it with "God over all, and blest eternally," cannot be verified.

7   On the approaches to the Trinity by the Campbells and Stone see Kelly D. Carter, *The Trinity in the Stone-Campbell Movement: Restoring the Heart of Christian Faith,* (Abilene, TX: Abilene Christian University Press, 2015), chapters 1-3.

8   Barton Stone, *The Christian Messenger,* (July 1830), 4:169.

9   Stone, *Christian Messenger,* 4:171.

creeds as a child in the Episcopal Church. In other words, I was a trinitarian before I was a Disciple, and I haven't found a reason to jettison that confession of faith since joining with the Disciples. Nonetheless, I understand why others have chosen to remain aloof from the doctrine. If you want to be strictly biblical, there is that lack of explicit trinitarian language (including the word Trinity) in the New Testament. I also realize that many Disciples find the doctrine to be a mere abstraction, as was expressed by Edward Scribner Ames. In response, I would simply ask: why did early Christians move toward a trinitarian understanding of God? What is it about Jesus and the Holy Spirit that called forth this development? Why did the confession of Jesus' divine nature come to the fore? Theologians such as Athanasius believed that salvation depended on Christ being fully divine so that what is mortal might become immortal. He wrote: "For he was made man that we might be made God; and he manifested himself by a body that we might receive the idea of the unseen Father; and he endured the insolence of men that we might inherit immortality."[10]

The creeds emerged as the Christian community sought to find a theological consensus upon which to unite, for they discovered that the Scriptures lent themselves to differing interpretations. They faced the reality that the Christian faith was rooted in a monotheistic tradition, but that they had come to understand Jesus to be in some way divine. They believed this concept was present in the New Testament, but they were not of one mind as to how this should be interpreted. Perhaps with some urging from the state, they looked for that consensus. The Stone-Campbell Movement, of which the Christian Church (Disciples of Christ) is one branch, has chosen not to embrace the creeds as authoritative statements, preferring to rest the case for Christian unity in Scripture. But this presents a problem, since Scripture, while normative, is open to

---

10   Athanasius, "On the Incarnation," in *Christology of the Later Fathers (Library of Christian Classics: Ichthus Edition)*, Edward R. Handy, ed., (Philadelphia: Westminster Press, 1954), pp. 107-108.

interpretation. So, we are back where the early Christians began, seeking consensus on which to build unity.

The question that faces my own tradition, the Christian Church (Disciples of Christ), concerns our confession of faith in God. If the vast majority of Christians, at least by confession, affirm the premise of the trinitarian nature of God, and many Disciples have shied away from fully embracing this confession, then who is God for us? In relationship to that question, what do we say about Jesus? Do we embrace the divinity of Christ or do we leave up to each individual or is it an irrelevant question? The founding generation of the Disciples chose to let the New Testament define the essence of the faith. So, is Jesus, as John would suggest, the Word (*logos*) made flesh? (Jn. 1:14). If so, what does that mean?

From experience, I know that there are Disciples who affirm the divinity of Christ and those who do not. Some amongst us want to affirm the humanity of Christ and believe that to stress divinity takes away from Jesus' humanity and his message. That is, the belief is that to affirm Christ's divine status puts our focus on the heavens at the cost of attention given to earthly matters, such as social justice. While there might be truth here, it is not a given that to affirm divinity is to neglect humanity.

The decision made at Chalcedon in 451 CE was that Jesus the Christ was fully divine and fully human—one person but two complete natures. To Enlightenment ears, this sounds illogical, but it served to keep in balance two confessions that had been made concerning Jesus' status as Son of God. The debate as to Jesus' identity continues to this day, but perhaps affirming the definition of Chalcedon can offer a way out, allowing us to affirm what ultimately transcends our human capacity to fully comprehend the divine. So, I wonder, does the Disciples discomfort with creedal statements inhibit unity? For if Scripture requires interpretation, on what will we unite? If unity is our polar star as Barton Stone intimated, what is the touchstone of that unity? If there is to be unity in the essentials, with liberty in the non-essentials, what are

4

the essentials? On what basis do we make that determination? Even if we were to affirm only that which is explicitly stated in Scripture as being binding, what of those explicit statements that give support to oppressive actions? So, simply relying on explicit biblical statements is insufficient. There is a need for discernment. Could tradition, along with reason, and experience, be useful in discerning what is good and true? If so, then might these three assists us in our conversations regarding the nature of God, including the apparent recognition of the church that the God revealed in the person of Jesus is both one and plural? As Alexander Campbell, himself, suggested, "the divine nature may be communicated or imparted in some sense; and, indeed, while it is essentially and necessarily singular, it is certainly plural in its personal manifestations. Hence, we have the Father, Son, and Holy Spirit equally divine, though personally distinct from each other. We have, in fact, but one God, one Lord, one Holy Spirit; yet these are equally possessed of one and the same divine nature."[11] Though Campbell eschewed creeds and even traditional trinitarian language, this is a trinitarian vision of God.

Who is Jesus in relationship to the Christian understanding of God? This was the question faced by the fourth-century church. With toleration, and then state-support, Christianity faced the prospect of welcoming an influx of new members, most of whom came into the church from polytheistic religious contexts. It became clear that that the church needed to have a common confession of faith to share with these new Christians. With the church existing in a variety of settings and speaking different languages, it became imperative that the churches begin defining their theological terms. This was especially true because different groups used similar language in different ways, which proved confusing. Thus,

---

11   Alexander Campbell, *The Christian System, in Reference to the Union of Christians, and a Restoration of Primitive Christianity, as Plead in the Current Reformation.* 4th edition. (Cincinnati: H.S. Bosworth, 1866; reprint, Salem, NH: Ayer Company, Publishers, 1988), p. 20.

creeds emerged as a response. The creeds, especially the Nicene Creed, sought to make sense of the confession of God's oneness as expressed in the *Shema*: *"Hear, O Israel: The Lord is our God, the Lord alone. You shall love the Lord your God with all your heart, and with all your soul, and with all your might"* (Deut. 6:4-5 NRSV), with texts that suggested that Jesus is the *Logos* or Word of God incarnate (John 1:1-14).

Although Campbell and Stone concluded that the creeds were more a hindrance than a help to their platform of unity (preferring to stick with the Bible, and more specifically the New Testament), this led to ambivalence about the Trinity and made substantive conversation about the God's nature and Christology difficult. I resonate with this word from Disciples theologian Joe Jones:

> Yet by discounting later church traditions, including creedal statements, the Restoration Movement deprived itself of the capacity to deal with differences within the New Testament discourses and practices. This became particularly painful with regard to how to interpret Jesus Christ. Wanting a Jesus without any creedal identification led to the Movement's divisive issue: in what sense is Jesus divine and in what sense human and in what sense our Savior? Incapacitated to develop and affirm any common confessional or creedal statement about Jesus, the Movement was left either to the dogmatic declarations of individual pastors and professors or to the dogma that only the individual believer can decide for herself who Jesus is—Jesus dissolved into the private preferences of the individual believer! Is it any wonder that a restoration movement of this character would find itself breaking apart into differing traditions?[12]

In other words, while the founders rejected creeds because they deemed them divisive, in the end, our lack of creeds may have made unity even more difficult to attain in the long term. Disciples

---

12   Joe R. Jones, *A Lover's Quarrel: A Theologian and His Beloved Church*, (Eugene, OR: Cascade Books, 2014), p. 16.

do have a foundational confession, and that is the Gospel, which is rooted in the life, death, and resurrection of Jesus. Nevertheless, could Joe Jones be correct in the following diagnosis? "While the Disciples wing has not been able to sustain a common trinitarian understanding of God, and the other wings are hesitant at the prospect, a nontrinitarian understanding will miss the mark and Jesus will be reduced to a prophet of some importance but not the incarnate life of God reconciling the world to Godself."[13]

13   Jones, *A Lover's Quarrel*, p. 19.

Chapter 2:

Campbell, Stone, and the Trinity

With Joe Jones' question in mind concerning whether Disciples noncreedalism could cause us to miss the mark on the question of Christ's nature, how might we have a substantive conversation about the Trinity, one that will unite and empower, rather than divide?[14] It seems to me that if we're to have this conversation, we need to start at the beginning with the Campbells (Thomas and Alexander) and Barton Stone. There is a fourth founder—Walter Scott—but he did not contribute much to this conversation, thus, we will focus on the Campbells and Stone.

Thomas and Alexander Campbell, along with Barton Stone, were products of their time. Their theology emerged out of a context that was influenced by Enlightenment thinkers such as John Locke, who argued for a "reasonable Christianity" that centered on the simple confession that Jesus was the Messiah. Like Barton Stone, Locke was accused of being a Socinian, and like Stone, he denied this charge. At the same time, neither Locke nor Stone was content to affirm the traditional confessions that emerged out of the fourth-century theological debates. In other words, the lack of a creed could explain much of the ambivalence on the part of the founders, who passed on that ambivalence to their progeny.

While Disciples have not taken a firm position on the Trinity, ecumenical conversations have at least made the Trinity a topic of conversation with Disciples circles. As a member of the World Council of Churches, Disciples have affirmed doctrinal standards that include an affirmation of the Trinity, for the Council defines itself as "a fellowship of churches which confess the Lord Jesus Christ as God and Saviour according to the scriptures, and there-

---

14   Jones, *A Lover's Quarrel,* p. 16.

fore seek to fulfill together their common calling to the glory of the one God, Father, Son and Holy Spirit."

As Ronald Osborn noted, Alexander Campbell refused to use the term Trinity because the term did not appear in the Bible, which led to the question of whether the Trinity has biblical support. Arius, the fourth century opponent of trinitarianism, insisted that the doctrine lacked such support. He could affirm a form of divinity for Christ, but not full divinity or equality with the Father. Others have been subtler in questioning Christ's equality and eternality with the Father divinity, but like Arius, they have found the doctrine difficult to accept.

While Campbell was loath to use the term Trinity, it is clear that he embraced the doctrine, as we noted earlier from his book *The Christian System*. By writing "we have the Father, Son, and Holy Spirit equally divine, though personally distinct from each other. We have, in fact, but one God, one Lord, one Holy Spirit; yes, these are equally possessed of one and the same divine nature," Campbell clearly affirms a traditional trinitarian formula.[15] At the same time, writing in *The Christian Baptist*, he objected to the "Calvinistic doctrine of the Trinity," because it "confounds things human and divine, and gives new ideas to bible terms unthought of by the inspired writers." One of the ideas that Campbell found especially vexing was the pre-existence of the Son of God, an idea required by most trinitarian theologies. Campbell insisted that "there was no Jesus . . . no Son of God, no Only Begotten, before the reign of Augustus Caesar. The relation that was before the Christian era was not that of a son and a father, terms which always imply disparity." On the other hand, he did believe that the *Logos* or Word of God existed from eternity and thus shared equality with God (who did not become the Father until Christ's human birth).[16] Without

---

15   Campbell, *Christian System*, p. 20.
16   Alexander Campbell, *A Compend of Alexander Campbell's Theology*, Royal Humbert, ed., (St. Louis: Bethany, 1961), pp. 94-98.

the traditional trinitarian language, Campbell found it difficult to clearly confess his trinitarian beliefs.

While Campbell affirmed the substance of the Trinity without embracing much of the theological language undergirding it, the same could not be said for Barton Stone. In the second edition of his *An Address to the Christian Churches in Kentucky, Tennessee & Ohio*—first published in 1814 and revised in 1821—Stone addressed directly the doctrine of the Trinity, which he found unintelligible and unnecessary.

> The doctrine of Trinity has long been a subject of endless controversy among theologians. I have thought the contest a war of words, while the combatants believed the same thing; seeing they all maintain the divine unity. On this doctrine many things are said, which are dark, unintelligible, unscriptural, and too mysterious for comprehension. Many of these expressions we have rejected; and for this reason we are charged with denying the doctrine itself. I shall state the doctrine, as generally stated and defended by our brethren, who oppose us, and give my reasons why I cannot receive it.[17]

Stone would later respond to Alexander Campbell's suggestion that they were brothers in Christ because they both worshiped Jesus as the only God in the universe, accusing Campbell of misunderstanding his beliefs regarding Jesus. He claimed to hold only to what Scripture revealed, and in his view, Scripture did not reveal that Jesus was the only God in the universe. As for being Arian or Unitarian, Stone would not admit to those terms either, though he does note that the Christians in the East (the Christian Connection), had accepted that designation, which proved disturbing to some in the West.[18]

---

17 Barton Stone, *An Address to the Christian Churches in Kentucky, Tennessee & Ohio on Several Important Doctrines of Religion. Second Edition— Corrected and Enlarged,* (Lexington, KY, 1821). http://www.piney.com/ Barton.W.Stone.Address.Christian.Churches.html

18 Barton Stone, *The Christian Messenger,* (November 1827), 2:10-13.

Kelly Carter suggests that Stone, who was influenced by his reading of *The Scripture Doctrine of the Trinity* written by the eighteenth-century heterodox Anglican theologian Samuel Clarke, might be best described as a "quasi-Arian." Like Clarke, Stone spoke of Jesus deriving his nature from the Father, therefore Jesus was not a created being.[19] If, as Carter clearly demonstrates, Stone followed the lead of Samuel Clarke in his understanding of the relationship of the Son to the Father, it might be better to speak of Stone not as a quasi-Arian, but as a Eusebian. As Thomas Pfizenmaier has demonstrated, Clarke's treatment of the Trinity reflects the Eusebian or *homoiousion* perspective, one that was prominent in the eastern churches during the fourth century. Pfizenmaier has shown that our understanding of Clarke's views is hindered by assuming there are only three possible positions on the Trinity—the Athanasian (affirming the full divinity of Jesus), the Arian (Jesus as created being and thus not divine), and the Sabellian (modalistic monarchianism, in which Jesus is understood to be an exalted human being). Clarke fit in none of these camps. He was clearly not an Athanasian, but he also denied being an Arian or a Socinian (Sabellian). By adding a fourth category, the Eusebian, we get a better understanding of Clarke's views, and I would add, Stone's as well. The Eusebian position (*homoiousion*), favored by many eastern bishops in the fourth century as an alternative to the Athanasian position, which some feared led to modalism, suggests that the Christ was divine, sharing like substance with the Father, but not the same substance. In other words, the Son stands subordinate to the Father. If my reading of Pfizenmaier is correct, Stone's Christology is similar enough to that of Samuel Clarke, which leads to the conclusion that he is much closer to orthodox trinitarianism than even he may have believed.[20]

---

19 Carter, *The Trinity in the Stone-Campbell Movement*, pp. 172-175.
20 Thomas C. Pfizenmaier, *The Trinitarian Theology of Dr. Samuel Clarke (1675-1729): Context, Sources, and Controversy,* (Leiden: Brill, 1997), pp. 139-141.

Despite their differences in theology Stone and Campbell found a way to unite their movements into one fellowship. Unfortunately, this movement that made unity a hallmark of its message has struggled to remain united as one fellowship. We seem to have chosen different elements of the founding vision to emphasize, whether restoring New Testament patterns of church governance or ecumenical relationships, all the while eschewing serious conversation about the Trinity.

In arguing for a more substantive conversation about the Trinity, I am not suggesting Disciples make the affirmation of the Trinity a test of fellowship. At the same time, I agree with Joe Jones that this makes it more difficult for us to converse about Jesus' identity, which has other consequences for us. When it came to finding a path to unity, Campbell and Stone chose to root their agreements in what was explicitly revealed in the New Testament. They were correct in their assumption that much of the vocabulary that undergirds trinitarian doctrine is not found in the Bible. This vocabulary evolved over time, as Christian theologians sought to make sense of the biblical revelation and their own experience of God, in light of new contexts—such as the move from Greek to Latin speaking regions.

There are very few verses of scripture that offer either explicit or implicit expression of a trinitarian formula. The two most explicit statements that can be interpreted in a trinitarian way are Matthew 28:19 and 2 Corinthians 13:13, but these were not enough to convince Stone that the Trinity is a biblical concept. Stone responded to those who claimed biblical support for the doctrine that they offered "a few scriptures of doubtful interpretation . . . on which is their entire reliance."[21] Yet, as Leonard Allen points out, "a three-fold pattern of divine relationality permeates the New Testament." It wasn't simply a philosophical construct but is rooted in the "necessary work of filling out the New Testament's pervasive triadic language about God as the gospel mission engaged

21   Barton Stone, *The Christian Messenger*, (July 1830), 4:169).

12

Greco-Roman culture."[22] Since at least the third century, Christian theologians had been reading scripture in a Trinitarian manner. This is true of both the New Testament and the Hebrew Bible. As they have done this, they have found sufficient evidence for the Trinity—consider the story of the three visitors to Abraham and Sarah at the Oak of Mamre. What posed a problem for Stone and Campbell was the absence of explicit trinitarian statements. However, their reluctance to read these passages in a trinitarian fashion may reflect their Enlightenment ethos. That fact may have closed off avenues of exploration that we might want to revisit.

If you are trinitarian, all hope is not lost. This is because there are many verses of Scripture that make sense when read in a trinitarian manner, which in fact Campbell did. Brevard Childs puts the issue in this way:

> It is a formulation of the church in its attempt to reflect faithfully on the biblical witness. But it was precisely by observing the unity and differentiation of God within the biblical revelation that the church was confronted with the Trinity. The divine subject, predicate and object, are not only to be equated but also differentiated. Indeed, it is the doctrine of the Trinity which makes the doctrine of God actually Christian.[23]

Ultimately, as we will see, the need for a doctrine of the Trinity ultimately arose from the need to make sense of the church's affirmation of the divine sonship of Jesus Christ. The doctrine emerged from the need to "do justice to the Christ who was from the church's inception confessed as Lord." As Childs also notes, when nineteenth-century Christians lost interest in the doctrine of the Trinity their Christologies also began to blur and become distorted.[24]

In the years following the passing of Stone and Campbell, there is little evidence of interest on the part of Disciples in the

---

22   Allen, *Poured Out,* p. 59-60, 63.
23   Childs, *Biblical Theology,* 375.
24   Childs, *Biblical Theology,* p. 376.

Trinity. There would be occasional engagements, like that of William Robinson, a British Disciple, but his engagement came in part from the influence of Karl Barth and his involvement in ecumenical conversations in Britain. Robinson roots his discussion of the Trinity in the premise that God is love, which "involves the notion of fellowship in the Godhead." He writes of what he calls the "Supra-personal" nature of God: "In the Christian experience, this develops into the knowledge of God as Father, Son, and Holy Spirit—the Doctrine of the Trinity."[25] More recently, both Joe Jones and Clark Williamson have embraced trinitarian understandings in their theological work. Among younger scholars, Peter Goodwin Heltzel has called for the development of a "robust Trinitarian theology." He argues that "embracing a theology of singing the Trinity, drawing on the deep trinitarian streams of the ecumenical tradition of twentieth-century ecumenism, provides a way for Disciples to continue to embrace and live into the Doctrine of the Trinity. As we sing the Trinity together we perform 'unity in diversity' in our new postcolonial age."[26] Campbell and Stone sought to define faith in biblical terms, hoping that this would be a platform for Christian unity. Could we have reached the point where embracing a creedal consensus might be necessary to achieve the same goal?

---

25   Robinson, *Whither Theology*, p. 53.
26   Peter Goodwin Heltzel, "Singing the Trinity," in *Chalice Introduction to Disciples Theology*, (St. Louis: Chalice Press, 2008), pp. 92ff.

Chapter 3:

The Bible, Tradition, and the Development of Trinitarian Vocabulary

Trinity and the Bible

This is not the place to go into depth regarding the question of the biblical roots of the doctrine of the Trinity. However, for Disciples, who trace their theological lineage to the Campbells and Barton Stone, we cannot ignore the question. While Alexander Campbell placed more weight on the New Testament than the Old Testament, a truly Christian theology must acknowledge its roots in the Hebrew Bible (lest we find ourselves in the Marcionite camp). The foundational message of the Hebrew Bible is that God is one. This is the message of the *Shema,* the Jewish confession of faith: "Hear, O Israel: The Lord is our God, the Lord alone. *You shall love the Lord your God with all your heart, and with all your soul, and with all your might"* (Deut. 6:4-5). The question for Christians is whether this declaration allows for any form of plurality within God's oneness. Veli-Matti Karkkainen suggests that for the people of Israel, the issue wasn't number but loyalty, with that in mind they were able to affirm the oneness of God and allow for some form of plurality. We see this in the use of Wisdom, Word, and Spirit regarding the way one encounters the one God.

So, what do we mean when speaking of a plurality with regard to the God of the OT? It is an incipient plurality within the one God, expressed in terms of "Wisdom," "Word," and "Spirit." These three seem to serve as (semi-)personified agents of divine activity. And very importantly, the existence

17

of such personified agents was not seen necessarily as a threat to monotheism.[27]

In a pre-critical age, Christian theologians were very adept at finding trinitarian threads in the Hebrew Bible. This was assisted by the use of the allegorical method of interpretation, which allowed for a deeper and broader reading of texts. Critical and historical study of scripture has raised questions about pre-critical methods of interpretation, which makes the process more difficult. In addition, engagement with Jewish scholars has also raised cautions about reading into the texts theologies that might not have been there originally. This includes the acknowledgment that Judaism is not trinitarian. At the same time, Christians assume and affirm that the God of Judaism is the same God as the God of Christianity. If this is true, then, as Miroslav Volf suggests, the same could be said of Islam. So, while Jews and Muslims hold to a more radical monotheism, Christians can affirm that the three traditions worship the same God, even if Christians affirm the Trinity. By affirming the shared belief in the one God, that doesn't mean the Trinity is an optional add-on. It is, "the full reality of the one God who, Christians affirm, can be worshipped, but only inadequately without reference to God's trinitarian nature." That is because if we take away the Trinity, then the Christian affirmation of the incarnation collapses, "and with it the whole Christian faith."[28] We might put it a bit differently: if Jesus is not the incarnate one, but rather one prophet among many, then perhaps we should embrace Islam.

With these cautions in mind, we can explore texts like Genesis 1:26, which has proven especially intriguing for Christian reflection. The use of the plural in the phrase "let us make human kind in our image, according to our likeness" is at least suggestive of some

27 Veli-Matti Karkkainen, *Christian Understandings of the Trinity: The Historical Trajectory,* (Minneapolis: Fortress Press, 2017), p. 11 (Kindle Edition).

28 Miroslav Volf, *Allah: A Christian Response,* (San Francisco: Harper One, 2011), p. 135.

form of plurality within God's nature. Theologians have wondered what the word "our" means. Now, it is doubtful that the author(s) had the Trinity in mind, but could the seeds be there? Is it appropriate for Christians to make use of this phrase in developing a trinitarian theology?

While we must admit that there is no direct reference to the Trinity in the Hebrew Bible, there are passages that offer us a foundation for a fruitful theological conversation. This is especially true of passages that speak of "Wisdom," which is often personalized in the Psalms and Proverbs as "Divine Wisdom." Wisdom is usually conceived of in feminine terms. Wisdom is often depicted as being involved in the creation of all things (Prov. 1:20-23; 9:1-6; Job 28; Ecclesiastes 24). There is the concept of "Word," or divine speech, which at times is personified (Ps. 119:89; Ps. 147:15-20; Is. 55:10-11). And then there is the "Spirit of God," who is depicted often as God's presence in the world, active in creation (Gen. 1:2); present in the life of the promised Messiah (Isa. 42:1-3); and as an agent of new creation (Ezek. 36:26; 37:1-14). There is also the concept of *Shekinah* (another word that is feminine in nature), that describes the means of God's dwelling in the world (Exodus 25:8; 43:9; Zech. 2:10; 8:3). These passages don't make for a doctrine of the Trinity, but they leave open the possibility of a broader understanding of God's nature. What we need to remember is that whatever understanding we might have of these concepts and similar concepts, they must be understood in the context of the Old Testament insistence on the oneness or unity of God (Deut. 6:4-5).

While it is understandable that the Hebrew Bible might have few if any explicit trinitarian declarations, one might expect the New Testament to be more forthcoming. However, even here there are no explicit statements of trinitarian doctrine. The doctrine is a theological construction that attempts to make sense of the biblical witness, especially those texts that affirm the primary relationship between Father and Son. The most explicit statement is the baptismal formula found in Matthew 28:19. In the Great Commission,

Jesus commands his followers to make disciples, baptizing them in the name of the Father, Son, and Holy Spirit. While this is the only New Testament expression of this formula, it has become the standard formula for most churches. A second passage, 2 Corinthians 13:13 (14), is more helpful in defining the relationship, but it's not without its own difficulties. The declaration is: "The grace of the Lord Jesus Christ, the love of God, and the communion of the Holy Spirit be with all of you." In Romans 8:11 we see implicit reference to a plurality within God regarding the resurrection: "If the Spirit of him who raised Jesus from the dead dwells in you, he who raised Christ from the dead will give life to your mortal bodies also through his Spirit that dwells in you."

Barton Stone is correct— "that there is but one living and true God, is a plain doctrine of revelation. 'We know that an Idol is nothing in the world, and that there is *none other God but one*. For though there be that are called Gods, whether in Heaven or in earth (as there be Gods many and Lords many). But to us there is *but one God*, the Father, of whom are all things, and we in him; and one Lord, Jesus Christ, by whom are all things, and we by him.' 1 Cor. 8, 4-6. Also Deut. 6, 4. Mark 12, 29, &c."[29] All Christians agree on the oneness of God. We hold this belief in common with our Jewish and Muslim kin, and yet the doctrine of the Trinity emerged from the Scriptural witness to a more complex understanding of that oneness. Veli Matti Karkkainen, suggests we avoid trying to find prooftexts and attend to the basic issue at hand: "So, what we have is this: on the one hand, the doctrine of the Trinity cannot be found even in the NT; on the other hand, Jesus's unique relation to the Father calls for an explanation that really takes us beyond the boundaries of the OT."[30] It is the relationship of the Father to Jesus that calls forth further reflection.

---

29   Stone, *Address to the Christian Churches*, http://www.piney.com/
      Barton.W.Stone.Address.Christian.Churches.html
30   Karkkainen, *Christian Understandings of the Trinity*, p. 16.

While we might wish there were explicit definitions of the Trinity to be found in the New Testament, affirmations of the full divinity of Christ and the person of the Holy Spirit required further development. While the fourth-century formulations might not be perfect, they have stood the test of time. Theologian Elizabeth Johnson captures the vision that the doctrine Trinity engenders in Christian theology:

> At its most basic the symbol of the Trinity evokes a liv-ingness in God, a dynamic coming and going with the world that points to an inner divine circling around in unimaginable relation. God's relatedness to the world in creating, redeem-ing, and renewing activity suggests to the Christian mind that God's own being is somehow similarly differentiated. Not an isolated, static, ruling monarch but a relational, dynamic, trip-ersonal mystery of love—who would not opt for the latter? [31]

The Historical Development of a Trinitarian Vocabulary

As we have noted, Alexander Campbell and Barton Stone had concerns about the dependence on non-biblical language to define and describe the doctrine of the Trinity. They wanted to use biblical language to define their theological positions. This proved difficult, and it was a significant reason why Stone wouldn't embrace the doc-trine of the Trinity. While it is true that much trinitarian vocabulary emerged over time, it emerged from early Christian reflection on the New Testament. This is especially true of the word *logos,* who was understood to be incarnate in the person of Jesus. Second-cen-tury writers, like Justin and Athenagoras, often spoke of the *Logos* and the Spirit in subordinate ways, but they linked both with God, not as creatures but as expressions of God's nature. What these early theologians discovered was that they needed a new vocabulary to

---

31   Elizabeth A. Johnson, *She Who Is: The Mystery of God in Feminist Theological Discourse.* (New York: The Crossroad Publishing Company, 2002), p. 192.

express what they found in Scripture. Many of the terms that we use today to speak of the Trinity, including the word *trinitas,* came into use as the church spread into Latin-speaking regions, requiring translation of Greek terms into Latin. This occurred not without some difficulty, but a vocabulary deemed acceptable by most if not all Christians was adopted.

One of the most important contributors to this development was Tertullian, the North African theologian of the early third century CE. He was a brilliant theologian and apologist for the church, and we look to him for many of the terms that the church came to use to describe God. These terms include the Latin word *trinitas.* He also introduced the term substance (the Latin *substantia* translates the Greek *ousia*) to describe the essence of God. Speaking in trinitarian terms, Father, Son, and Holy Spirit share one substance. The third term was *persona,* which he used to translate the Greek *hypostasis.* God is one in substance but still is encountered as three persons.

The next stage in the process came at the Council of Nicaea, which addressed conflicting understandings of the Trinity that had emerged in Alexandria. While neither Arius nor Athanasius spoke at the council, it was their conflicting theological work that drove the conversation that led to the development of what became the normative definitions of God's nature. Although the position espoused by Athanasius would become that normative definition, it took most of the century to reach a consensus. The question raised by Arius had to do with whether the Son shared the same substance as the Father. Arius denied that Jesus shared full divinity, insisting that his view was the more biblical position. The term that was embraced by the council of Constantinople in 381 to define the relationship of Father and Son was *homoousious* (of the same substance). What began at Nicaea in 325 CE and ended at the Council of Constantinople in 381 CE was the adoption of *homoousious,* and the promulgation of a creed that would express this consensus. While this became the consensus, that doesn't mean everyone was comfortable with the term. In part, this had to do with language differences. Greek and Latin theologians struggled with their language, but what Nicaea and Constantinople did was create a common affirmation that embraced both the principle that God is one and recognized the plurality that exists within that oneness. They named this plurality Father, Son, and Holy Spirit. Sticking with "biblical" language, while honorable, was found to be less than helpful. We can see this present in Alexander Campbell's own struggles to speak of the Trinity in biblical terms.

CHAPTER 4:

WAYS OF APPROACHING THE TRINITY

Although the foundational trinitarian vocabulary was introduced in the third and fourth centuries, the conversation as to the nature and purpose of the doctrine of the Trinity continues to this day. Indeed, among Disciples, one will find partisans of both Athanasius and Arius in our pews and in our pulpits, even if those names are not attached. When it comes to trinitarian theology, there are essentially two ways of approaching this question. On one hand, we can talk about the economic Trinity, and on the other the immanent Trinity. These approaches are not mutually exclusive, but rather two sides of one coin. One perspective focuses on God's external activity in bringing salvation to creation, and the other on God's internal identity. Both ways of approaching the question rely on the same formula that was espoused at Nicaea and later at Constantinople in the fourth century.

As a Disciple, I have found the trinitarian musings of Joe Jones and Clark Williamson helpful. They do theology from different perspectives, but we can learn from both of them as we consider whether it is possible for Disciples to pursue a trinitarian understanding of God. I should note that I find myself closer to Jones in my own theology but appreciate both.

Jones believes that when it comes to understanding the Trinity, we should distinguish between God's essence and God's actuality. Failure to do so has important consequences for our understanding of trinitarian doctrine. Jones places himself between classical theism and process theism, a position that I find myself in as well. Williamson is influenced by both Paul Tillich and Process Theology, and he explicitly does theology from a post-holocaust perspective. Yet, both affirm the Trinitarian conception of God.

The Economic Trinity

We can start with the economic Trinity because this is the way we encounter God as Trinity. Jones writes that "relying on the authoritative priority of the biblical testimony, the term 'economic Trinity' refers to God's acts of self-communicating disclosure in the history of Israel and of Jesus Christ and the calling of the church. It is the *oikonomia* of God's disclosive management of salvation history in creation history."[32] To speak of the "economic Trinity" is to speak of the ways in which God discloses God's self to us in Christ and through the Holy Spirit, which leads to salvation or the healing of creation. Therefore, when we talk of the economic Trinity, we're talking about God's role in the creation, redemption, and sanctification of the created order. These three activities, however, should not be seen as occurring sequentially. Clark Williamson's theological orientation differs from Jones (he moves in a Process direction), but he helps us understand the way in which God encounters creation as Trinity, so that "in each moment of our lives God creates us anew, redeems us out of the narrowness and stupidity of the past, and calls us forward toward God's future with all God's friends."[33] Jones notes that it is ultimately the incarnation that moves us toward trinitarian reflection, for it is the incarnation that truly reveals differentiation within God's nature. If we affirm the singular identification of Jesus with Israel's God, then "it becomes impossible to identify adequately who God is apart from some triune way of understanding that includes Jesus and the Spirit and grasps the otherness within God's actuality."[34]

When we think about the trinitarian nature of God, one of the more intriguing images is that of the three visitors whom Abraham and Sarah encounter at the Oaks of Mamre (Genesis 18:1-15).

---

32   Joe R. Jones, *On Being the Church of Jesus Christ in Tumultuous Times*, (Eugene, OR: Cascade Books, 2005), p. 125.

33   Clark Williamson, *Way of Blessing, Way of Life: A Christian Theology*, (St. Louis: Chalice Press, 1999), p. 118.

34   Jones, *On Being the Church of Jesus Christ*, p. 126.

Clark Williamson draws on this story that emphasizes hospitality to suggest that "the Trinity is a communion of equal persons (coequal, the tradition liked to say), and we are invited into such communion." He goes on to say:

> We speak of God as one in order to make clear that God is not divided, not double-minded. We speak of God as three to affirm communion in God. Life is a blessing and well-being when all relations of domination and oppression are expelled. Communion among persons is the divine order and the intended human order of well-being. The fundamental intent of the doctrine of the Trinity is to protect an understanding of God as a profound relational communion. A relationship (not merely a relation) of authentic communion among God, human beings, and all God's creatures is the aim of God's work in the world.[35]

There is much more to be said about the Trinity. It is a concept that is full of possibilities. What I've shared so far is an expression of the "economic Trinity." When we encounter God, we don't encounter God's inner being, we encounter God as God engages us, bringing shalom, which is healing, wholeness, salvation.

The Immanent Trinity

When we speak of God's essence, we speak in terms of the "immanent Trinity." As Joe Jones reminds us "everything we say about the immanent Trinity is derived from what we say about the economic Trinity."[36] This side of the equation is a reminder that God is Triune in God's essence, and not only in the actions of salvation history. This perspective on God's nature is a way of steering clear of modalism. That is, viewing God in terms of three modes of being that changes from situation to situation. Thus, God starts out as Creator, becomes Redeemer, and then the Sustainer.

---

35   Williamson, *Way of Blessing*, pp. 126-127.
36   Jones, *Grammar of Christian Faith*, 1:212-213.

Some theologians use the term *perichoresis*—the mutual indwelling of persons—to explain the interrelationship of the three persons of the Trinity. This concept emerged in the eighth century with John of Damascus as a way of expressing the unity of God not in the person of the Father but in the relationship of the three persons of the Trinity. Catherine Mowry LaCugna writes that this "expressed the idea that the three divine persons mutually inhere in one another, draw life from one another, 'are' what they are by relation to one another." She further writes that while there is no confusion between persons, there is also no separation. There is in this model complete interdependence. She writes further: "The model of *perichoresis* avoids the pitfalls of locating the divine unity either in the divine substance (Latin) or exclusively in the person of the Father (Greek), and locates unity instead in diversity, in a true *communion of persons*."[37] This concept is present as well in Jürgen Moltmann's concept of a social or open Trinity. He writes of this "perichoretic form of unity, . . . it cannot be realized by a single subject alone, and cannot be thought without the three divine Persons. Their shared nature, their shared consciousness, and their shared will is formed intersubjectively through their specific personhood in each case, by their specific consciousness in each case, and by their own will in each case."[38]

There has been a renaissance in trinitarian thinking in recent decades, much of which has been traced to Karl Barth. For the most part, Disciples have not been actively engaged in that conversation, with perhaps the exception of a few, such as Joe Jones and Clark Williamson. As Veli Matti Karkkainen has noted the Enlightenment project largely suppressed trinitarian thinking. The Campbells and Stone were influenced by figures of the Enlighten-

---

37   Catherine Mowry LaCugna, *God for Us: The Trinity & Christian Life*, (San Francisco: HarperOne, 1991), pp. 270-271.

38   Jürgen Moltmann, *Experiences in Theology: Ways and Forms of Christian Theology*, Margaret Kohl, trans., (Minneapolis: Fortress Press, 2000), p. 322.

ment, including John Locke, who sought to move away from the creedal language and rest solely in the Bible, which led to muted views of the Trinity at best. Stone was influenced by Samuel Clarke, whose trinitarian understandings were deemed heterodox. There were conservative theologians such as Charles Hodge that tried to defend the Trinity, but it was clearly a doctrine in decline during the eighteenth and nineteenth centuries.[39]

Speaking of the Trinity Today

So, how do we speak of God today? Many raise questions about the usefulness of Trinitarian language, especially in its traditional formulation. Naming God as Father, Son, and Holy Spirit can suggest that God is male and that males are superior to women. Even if we consider the Holy Spirit in feminine terms, this can easily lead to a top-down hierarchy that leaves not only the Son as second in line, but the Spirit as a third person, and sort of an afterthought. One of the recent formulas that has gained popularity is Creator, Redeemer, Sustainer/Sanctifier. While this is attractive, it has the look of modalism. In other words, what we have are three job descriptions, not three persons. Traditionally it has been held that "external works of God are indivisible," thus Father, Son, and Spirit engage in the act of creation.

The traditional trinitarian formula has a biblical foundation (Matthew 28:19-20), which means it has tradition at its back. It also speaks in relational terms, especially regarding Father and Son. The language used to express the doctrine of the Trinity is also highly masculine, which has in many cases lent support to efforts to suppress the role of women in the church and society. It could lead to the belief that God is male, and as Mary Daly famously declared "if God is male, then the male is God." This leads to recognition, as Elizabeth Johnson suggests: "At this point in the living tradition I believe that we need a strong dose of explicitly female imagery

---

39   Karkkainen, *Christian Understandings of the Trinity,* 172-175.

to break the unconscious sway that male trinitarian imagery holds over the imaginations of even the most sophisticated thinkers."[40] The fact is, Scripture has a significant store of female images for God, including Holy Wisdom. This storehouse could help us begin to re-envision the Trinity in forms that challenge male dominance, without ending up with modalism.

Elizabeth Johnson, who is Roman Catholic, suggests the use of *Sophia* or wisdom as a means of reformulating the Trinity so that we encounter the "unoriginated Mother, her beloved Child, and the Spirit of their mutual love."[41] She offers other symbols of the Trinity, but the point is reimagining our language for God in ways that are faithful to the tradition, and yet expand our horizons. Clark Williamson, following William Placher, suggests another possible solution to the present dilemma, the formula: "Father, Son, and Holy Spirit, Mother of us All."[42] Ultimately, the challenge for us as we move forward is to keep in mind the importance of relationality in our understandings of God's nature, both God's external (economic) relationship with humanity, and God's internal relationality.

Even as we wrestle with the question of finding new ways of naming God that are faithful to the tradition, and yet inclusive, we are facing another challenge. That challenge comes from the increasing numbers of interfaith conversations. Trinitarian language has presented challenges, for both Jews and Muslims have much stricter monotheism. This language can be a stumbling block to these important conversations as well. Yet, as Miroslav Volf argues in his book *Allah,* we can have a fruitful conversation, for Christians as well as Jews and Muslims affirm the premise that God is one. We may differ in our understanding of that oneness, but not on the premise of unity. At the same time, it requires humility on all sides to admit that our language for God is inadequate to

40   Johnson, *She Who Is,* p. 212.
41   Johnson, *She Who Is,* pp. 214-215.
42   Williamson, *Way of Blessing,* p. 115.

God's full reality.[43] It might make things easier if we abandoned the Trinity, but is this the best choice? Would this involve setting aside Christian theology in the pursuit of some form of common confession? Is this the most faithful way of engaging in interfaith dialog? As Joe Jones writes "it is clear that Christians should not pretend to converse and speak from some position *above* Christian faith; they should speak honestly as Christians *from* the Christian perspective. But from that perspective, this affirmation is crucial: all the people of the other traditions of religion are our brothers and sisters, created by God, loved by God, and ultimately redeemed by God."[44] While we may hold many things in common, it is the differences that make for the most fruitful conversations—and may help each of us gain a better understanding of our faith traditions as we put our faith into words.

---

43   Volf, *Allah*, pp. 127-148.
44   Jones, *Grammar of Christian Faith*, 1:99.

Chapter 5:

The Trinity and Non-Creedal Christianity

It must be admitted that the Trinity, as a doctrine, is rooted in inferences read from Scripture, including the premise that the Word was in the beginning with God, and in fact, is God, and that the Word became flesh and dwelt among us. Alexander Campbell was clear in that he believed that the *Logos* existed from eternity and that this Word became flesh in the person of Jesus. If God is one, and yet we have references to Jesus having some divine qualities, how should we speak of God? Over time, this led to the creation of rules of faith and creeds that served to summarize the growing witness to the Christian faith. Early Christians realized they needed to find vocabulary by which to express their faith and ended up setting down specific doctrines of the faith. The Nicene Creed is a reflection of this effort. Disciples of Christ are well known for their ambivalence regarding creeds, happily declaring that there is "no creed but Christ."

While the declaration that Jesus is the Christ and Son of God and Savior has been sufficient for Disciples when it comes to welcoming people into the community, we have left the definition of these terms open. Disciples do not see this confession being a test of fellowship, but it is a statement of allegiance. There is a simplicity here, especially as compared to other communities that require the embrace of a particular statement of faith or creed. Nonetheless, this confession suggests that there is a core of faith that defines the community.

When it comes to the more comprehensive statements of faith, such as the Nicene Creed, it is wise to recognize that they are not infallible, and the language of the confessions can change with time.

Since Christians continue to recite the Nicene and Apostles Creeds, even if the wording of these creeds are rooted in ancient Greek philosophical categories, suggests that these words have lasting value, even if not every word is taken literally.[45] They exist because they speak to a need. I would suggest that need is a starting point for considering what it means to be a Christian. What are the markers we might use to describe our faith?

The Christian Church (Disciples of Christ), along with the rest of their Stone-Campbell relatives, have chosen not to make creeds, including the Nicene Creed, a definitive statement of faith. Disciples have resisted creating doctrinal standards by which to judge one's orthodoxy. Stone and Campbell both pointed to the Bible and sought to rely on biblical terms to express their faith. While this seems commendable, it does present problems, for it limits vocabulary that one might use to confess their faith. We see this present in the attempts made by both Stone and Campbell to speak coherently of God's nature, especially regarding the Trinity. Campbell could find traces of the Trinity in Scripture, and this led him to affirm the doctrine of the Trinity in principle, but not in language. Unfortunately, that distinction has led to confusion. Barton Stone, on the other hand, found the doctrine so unwieldy that it strained what he believed accorded with logic. When combined his belief that Scripture clear support for the doctrine, he simply rejected it whole cloth (though as noted above, I do not believe he was as "heterodox" when it comes to the Trinity as previously believed).

I am of the belief that the church moved toward the doctrine of the Trinity because it made sense of the biblical testimony and the experience of the Christian community. As a historian, I can see why the church, as it reflected on Scripture and Christian experience of God, including the belief that Jesus was divine, devised

---

45   On the philosophical difficulties that the creedal statements present, as noted by one who questions the traditional understandings of the Trinity, see Chris Eyre, *A Holy Mystery: Taking Apart the Trinity,* (Gonzalez, FL: Energion Publications, 2019), pp. 19-23.

creeds to serve as guideposts for the church. They reflected a growing consensus as to how the church spoke of God in worship. It is true that they were used to enforce orthodoxy, but they also offered Christians a way of expressing their faith in summary form. In an age when most people were not literate but could memorize, this proved useful. I wonder whether, in our discomfort with creeds, along with a tradition of rejecting humanly devised speculative theologies, we have limited our ability to speak confidently of God. Perhaps Disciples, in their rejection of speculative theology, have failed to recognize our own theological presuppositions. As Dwight Stevenson notes, "The clear-cut division between the believing of the 'facts' of Scripture and the 'opinions' of theology is not clear-cut at all; no interpretation of the Bible can break free of human opinion and error."[46] The Founders believed Scripture was clear on matters of importance, but we have discovered that things are not quite that simple. We have also affirmed the right of each individual to embrace their own theology, but have given them the resources needed to make that determination.

Our discomfort with creeds is rooted in our Enlightenment origins. Stone and Campbell were the inheritors of a tradition that goes back to the seventeenth century. The Enlightenment project sought to limit metaphysical speculation, encouraging the use of scriptural language, and thus set aside creeds, or at least limit their use. John Locke, whose influence on the Stone-Campbell Movement was significant, argued for a reasonable Christianity that confessed Jesus to be the Son of God but could find nothing in Scripture about one God in three persons. Locke and Samuel Clarke, whom we have earlier encountered as an influence on Barton Stone, were not Deists. They emphasized reason, but they also affirmed the centrality of divine revelation (Scripture). At the

---

46 Dwight E. Stevenson, "Faith versus Theology in the Thought of the Disciple Fathers," in *The Reformation of Tradition (The Renewal of the Church: Panel of Scholars Reports)*, Ronald E. Osborn, ed., (St. Louis: The Bethany Press, 1963), p. 56.

same time, they found the creedal formulations at Nicaea and Constantinople to be problematic and wanted to stay with what was revealed in Scripture.

Although Disciples are heirs of the Enlightenment project, which led to a form of biblical primitivism, and an even starker rejection of Tradition than was true of the earlier Reformers, could this primitivism present its own challenges, especially in light of the challenge of the critical study of Scripture? As Ralph Wilburn writes: "the 'impregnable rock of scripture,' upon which classical Protestantism planted its feet, is not so impregnable any more, thanks to the science of biblical criticism."[47] If we no longer have an infallible Bible to draw from, then how might we formulate our faith? I for one affirm the primary authority of Scripture, but I also recognize that we cannot jettison two thousand years of reflection on that authority. We do not put our faith in dogma or creeds. They are not the object of faith, but they bear witness to Christian confession of faith in Christ. It would seem to me that if we keep the creeds in their proper place, not granting them infallibility, but allowing them to bear witness to the normative witness of Scripture, we can find words to express our faith in the God revealed in Jesus. It is here, in our attending to this witness that includes the creeds that we discover the Trinity as the Christian way of speaking of God. Might our historic discomfort with the creedal statements limit our ability to speak of God in ways that resonate with other members of the body of Christ?

As we consider the nature of God, a conversation that includes the name(s) we use, we must recognize that no name and no understanding can exhaust the possibilities. Thus, we must continue to push the boundaries. Whatever our theological formulas, they will not exhaust what we would confess as to who God might be.

---

47   Ralph G. Wilburn, "The Role of Tradition in the Church's Experience of Jesus as Christ," in *The Reconstruction of Theology (The Renewal of the Church: Panel of Scholars Reports)*, Ralph G. Wilburn, ed., (St. Louis: The Bethany Press, 1963), p. 109.

The current theological conversation regarding the Trinity illustrates this ongoing effort to move from faith to understanding, from experiencing the economic Trinity to better understanding the inner nature of God whom we confess to be one and yet whom experience as three persons. While Disciples embrace the principle of freedom in our theological conversations, our ecumenical and interfaith commitments call forth from us a witness that is coherent and faithful to the tradition that is rooted in Scripture.

I am a Disciple minister. As such, I embrace the principle of freedom that is deeply embedded in our denominational DNA. At the same time, having embraced an ecumenical spirit, that assumes that the spirit of the covenant that binds our Disciples community together extends beyond the boundaries of our denomination, I give heed to the broad witness of the historic church. It may not be a perfect witness, but to ignore that witness is a mark hubris. If we listen to the historic tradition (Tradition), then when it comes to the nature of God, the traditions of the historic church have consistently declared that God is one and yet three. Standing in this broad stream of Christian history, I find the doctrine of the Trinity to be the most compelling way of understanding the nature of God. As one who lives within the Disciples of Christ/Stone-Campbell tradition, I affirm our commitment to freedom. Therefore, an affirmation of this doctrine, should not be considered a test of fellowship. As William T. Moore, a Disciples historian and minister of an earlier generation wrote of Alexander Campbell's understandings of the Trinity and its place in defining the essentials of the faith:

> He was himself, at this very time and ever afterwards, largely in sympathy with those who call themselves Trinitarians. He also believed and taught the Supreme Deity of Jesus Christ, but he preferred to express the relations of the Godhead in Scriptural language rather than in the language of the

schools, and he utterly refused to make a test of fellowship of any speculation with respect to the matter.[48]

While, as a Disciples of Christ pastor and theologian (yes Disciples have theologians), I agree with Alexander Campbell that one's position on the Trinity should not be a test of fellowship. At the same time, it does us no favors as Disciples to use the shibboleth of human doctrine to stay clear of the conversation. If we are to be true to our ecumenical commitments, then it would seem appropriate to hear the witness of the ecumenical community on this matter.

I will close with these words from Clark Williamson regarding the intent of the doctrine of the economic Trinity. "The doctrine of the Trinity is a symbol that matures over time as a people reflect on their experience with the God of Israel disclosing God's self to them in Jesus Christ in the power of the Spirit."[49] This symbol has proven durable, even as it has faced numerous challenges, especially over the past three centuries. The fact that we have seen a resurgence of Trinitarian thinking over the past half-century, suggests that there is much more to learn about Jesus, about the Holy Spirit, about God in God's essence.

---

48   William Thomas Moore, *A Comprehensive History of the Disciples of Christ*, (SCM e-Prints. Kindle Edition), Loc. 3132.
49   Williamson, *Way of Blessing*, p. 123.

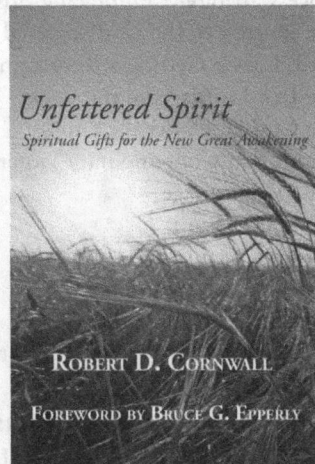

More from Energion Publications

Generous Quantity Discounts Available

Dealer Inquiries Welcome

Energion Publications — P.O. Box 841

Gonzalez, FL_ 32560

Website: http://energionpubs.com

Phone: (850) 525-3916

www.ingramcontent.com/pod-product-compliance
Lightning Source LLC
Chambersburg PA
CBHW011748020426
42331CB00014B/3324